365

Thoughts
for Daily
Meditation

WHITE STAR PUBLISHERS

365

Thoughts
for Daily
Meditation

CONTENTS

MINDFULNESS, OPENING HEART

Mindfulness means self-awareness. It is the ability to feel that we belong to the present moment, that we can seize the opportunities it offers, and so benefit from them. Moreover, it is the ability to face any difficult moment with a clear mind, freeing ourselves from anxieties.

Learning how to meditate, to breathe in harmony with the whole universe, even for a few minutes, enables us to acknowledge the potential for healing and transformation that we have within, paving the way to peace of mind and happiness.

However, mindfulness is more than just that. It aims to make us live each moment of our existence in an effortless and concentrated state of mind, without being vexed by past recollections, present pains, and anxieties for what lies ahead. Being able to perceive ourselves in our present time and space, in our "here and now," means to realize that we belong to Nature, and so share its tremendous strength, which sometimes we forget. Effortlessly following the endless flow of the seasons will prove beneficial to our well-being and will enable us to get once again into the rhythm of Nature, which the frenzy and psychological stress of the modern era are conspiring to suppress forever.

Learning how to meditate is important, but equally important is learning how to listen to our body and mind, and give Nature a prominent place in our life, recognizing her as a spiritual teacher who must be heeded and respected.

AND MIND TO NATURE

The acceptance of change, patience, resilience, a non-judging attitude, the ability to respond accordingly to every demand and need: these are just some of the teachings that Nature can offer, taking our hand on the path toward peacefulness.

Practicing mindfulness means developing empathy for the wholeness of which we are part, opening ourselves to the world, and establishing a mutually beneficial relationship with others. Today the power of mindfulness is acknowledged in many fields. Physicians recommend it to ease the stress and emotional burdens of their patients. Teachers recommend it to their teenage students to increase their focus and cognitive abilities, or simply to get through such a delicate period as adolescence. Companies turn to it to enhance the well-being of their employees, improve productivity, and generate harmony and satisfaction at the organizational level.

There are no preconditions of either age or gender to practice mindfulness, but an open heart and mind. However, we must have a guide, and Nature is the ultimate teacher to whom we must pay attention, learning to reciprocate her teachings and boons with loving care – above all now, in these present times of great ecological sufferings.

How can we begin? If we want to achieve a true relationship with Nature, let's start observing the world around us with a sympathetic attitude.

Since antiquity, human beings have looked at Nature as their common mother, and they have gleaned from her principles and inspiration. More inquisitive minds have been guided by her in their exploration of reality; more contemplative souls have taken shelter in her, seeking protection from the sufferings of life. Today, we increasingly hear experts talking about "eco-mindfulness," a form of active meditation in which regeneration and healing take shape in communion with Nature, by consciously breathing, moving and living in her. We can start with simple, ordinary things, like enjoying the benefits of a relaxing stroll in the woods, and then pass to more powerful emotions, such as those granted by the sun rising behind a mountain range, a sunset on the sea, a breathtaking view, or a violent storm. These are the easiest and most immediate means to free our mind from negativity, anxiety, and anguish, paving the way to a new and much needed self-awareness that will enable us to regain our balance and fulfil our positive potential.

Other powerful energies can be garnered if we change perspective from the big picture to the small details. Besides her grand and magnificent spectacles, Nature can equally inspire us with her little, overlooked, everyday marvels: the resilience of a robin darting from the snow in the

dead of winter, the gentle force of the snowdrop blooming at the begin-
ning of spring, the imposing strength of an oak in the middle of a forest,
the flexibility of a bending reed resisting the violence of the wind, the
perspicaciousness of the squirrel in managing resources, the wisdom of
the wolf, shrewd predator but also loving teacher of its cubs.

Our ancestors – whose bond with Nature was much stronger than
ours – considered these animals and plants as divine manifestations, and
their shamans found in them the key to comprehend the intimate nature
of the human being, arousing the power to heal both soul and body.
Back then, totemic animals embodied human characteristics, because our
ancestors recognized that everything, both living creatures and inanimate
objects, were part of Nature and so shared the same fundamental qualities.
Today, we can still contemplate Nature with the same attitude, learning
what we have to keep and what we must let go in our life, learning not
to ask for immediate and definitive answers to our problems, but to adapt
to changes effortlessly, considering them as opportunities to progress
in our journey.

It seems simple, and it can be so, once we accept that we belong to
Nature and are part of her infinite flowing.

1ST

January

There are only two days in the year that nothing can be done.
One is called Yesterday and the other is called Tomorrow.
Today is the right day to love, believe, do and mostly live.

– Tenzin Gyatso, 14th Dalai Lama

JANUARY

2ND

January

Stones sleep in the snow with green
dreams in their heart.

– Olav H. Hauge

3RD

January

Believe me, you will find more lessons in the
woods than in books. Trees and stones will
teach you what you cannot learn from masters.

– Bernard of Clairvaux

4TH

January

Wherever you go, there you are.

– *Thomas à Kempis*

5TH

January

Nature, to be commanded,
must be obeyed.

– *Francis Bacon*

6TH

January

Use what talent you possess: the woods
would be very silent if no birds sang
except those that sang best.

— Attributed to Henry Van Dyke

7TH

January

Life is a second-by-second miracle.

— Charlotte Joko Beck

8TH

January

The brightness of the snow
dims all our human greediness.

– Helena Anhava

9TH

January

Adopt the pace of nature:
her secret is patience.

– Ralph Waldo Emerson

10TH

January

Even in winter it shall be green
in my heart.

– Frédéric Chopin

11TH

January

Only in the winter, in the country,
can you have longer, quiet stretches
when you can savour belonging to yourself.

– Ruth Stout

12TH

January

Only in winter do the pine
and cypress show
they are evergreen.

– Confucius

13TH

January

Like a seed, my soul needs
the secret work of this season.

– Giuseppe Ungaretti

14TH

January

You, yourself, as much as anybody
in the entire universe, deserve your love
and affection.

– Buddha

15TH

January

In the midst of winter,
I found there was, within me,
an invincible summer.

– Albert Camus

16TH

January

In nature, nothing is perfect
and everything is perfect.
Trees can be contorted, bent in weird
ways, and they're still beautiful.

– *Alice Walker*

17TH

January

The snow and its magnificent silence.
There is nothing more deserving
of the name silence, than snow
on rooftops and across the ground.

– Erri De Luca

18TH

January

Life can only take place in the present
moment. If we lose the present
moment, we lose life.

– Buddha

19TH

January

In all things of nature there is something of the marvelous.

– Aristotle

20TH

January

Looking at beauty in the world is the first step
of purifying the mind.

– Amit Ray

21ST

January

When the winds of change blow, some people
build walls and others build windmills.

– Chinese proverb

22ND

January

How beautiful the Sun is when newly risen.
He hurls his morning greetings like an explosion!

– Charles Baudelaire

23RD

January

Nature does nothing in vain.

– Aristotle

24TH

January

Not a single thing is left out of the present moment.

– Eihei Dōgen

25TH

January

When we feel weak, all we have to do
is wait a little while. The spring returns
and the winter snows melt and fill us
with new energy.

– Paulo Coelho

26TH

January

Take care of each moment
and you take care of all time.

– Buddha

27TH

January

One must maintain a little bit
of summer, even in the middle
of winter.

– Henry David Thoreau

28TH

January

Stars are holes in the sky
from which the light
of the infinite shines.

– Confucius

29TH

January

Be glad of life because it gives you
the chance to love and to work
and to play and to look at the stars.

– Henry Van Dyke

30TH

January

If humanity is to survive,
happiness and inner equilibrium
are of the utmost importance.

– Tenzin Gyatso, 14th Dalai Lama

31ST

January

Time is like a snowflake; as we decide
what to make of it, it disappears.

– Romano Battaglia

1ST

February

There is one book which is open to everyone, the book of nature.
In this good and great volume, I learn to serve and adore its Author.

– Jean-Jacques Rousseau

FEBRUARY

2ND

February

The February sunshine steeps
your boughs and tints the buds
and swells the leaves within.

– William Cullen Bryant

3RD

February

To appreciate the beauty
of a snowflake it is necessary
to stand out in the cold.

– Aristotle

4TH

February

One may not reach the dawn save
by the path of the night.

– Kahlil Gibran

5TH

February

And each one sees
what in his bosom burns.

– Johann Wolfgang Goethe

6TH

February

Where does the rainbow end, in your soul
or on the horizon?

– Pablo Neruda

7TH

February

Look up to the sky. You'll never find rainbows
if you're looking down.

– Charlie Chaplin

8TH

February

Nothing will prevent the sun from rising again, even the darkest night.
Because beyond the black curtain of the night there is a dawn that awaits us.

– Kahlil Gibran

9TH
February

Night is never so black as before dawn,
but nonetheless dawn will always rise
to cancel its darkness.

– *Romano Battaglia*

10TH
February

I am lit with immensity.

– *Giuseppe Ungaretti*

11ᵀᴴ
February

The physician treats,
but nature heals.

– Hippocrates

12ᵀᴴ
February

Remember that nature
is the best physician.

– Galen

13TH

February

Love in the past is only a memory.
Love in the future is only a fantasy.
True love lives in the here and now.

– Buddha

14TH

February

When you arise in the morning,
think of what a precious privilege
it is to be alive, to breathe, to think,
to enjoy, to love.

– Marcus Aurelius

15TH

February

May your trails be crooked,
winding, lonesome, dangerous,
leading to the most amazing view.

– Edward Abbey

16TH

February

The wind blows wherever it pleases.
You hear its sound, but you cannot
tell where it comes from or where
it is going. So it is with everyone
born of the Spirit.

– Jesus of Nazareth

17TH

February

The primary indication of a well-ordered
mind is a man's ability to remain in one
place and linger in his own company.

– Lucius Annaeus Seneca

18TH

February

Knowledge is learning something
every day. Wisdom is letting go
of something every day.

– Zen proverb

19TH
February

Each of us must inquire in their own way, each of us must walk their own path, because the same place can mean different things to different travellers.

– Tiziano Terzani

20TH
February

Your breathing should flow gracefully, like a river and not like a chain of rugged mountains or the gallop of a horse.

– Thích Nhất Hạnh

21ST

February

Everything you can imagine,
nature has already created.

– Albert Einstein

22ND

February

Look deep, deep into nature, and then
you will understand everything better.

– Albert Einstein

23RD

February

Life is really simple, but we insist
on making it complicated.

– Confucius

24TH

February

The creatures that inhabit this earth – be they human beings or animals –
are here to contribute, each in its own particular way, to the beauty
and prosperity of the world.

– Tenzin Gyatso, 14th Dalai Lama

25TH
February

If you shape your life according
to nature, you will never be poor;
if according to people's opinions,
you will never be rich.

– Epicurus

26TH
February

Sometimes at night I would sleep
open-eyed underneath a sky dripping
with stars. I was alive then.

– Albert Camus

27TH
February

There is always in February some
one day, at least, when one smells
the yet distant, but surely coming, summer.

– Gertrude Jekyll

28TH/29TH
February

Clouds do not always darken the sky;
sometimes they illuminate it.

– Elsa Morante

1ST

March

And could you keep your heart in wonder at the daily miracles
of your life, your pain would not seem less wondrous than your joy.
And you would accept the seasons of your heart, even as you have
always accepted the seasons that pass over your fields.

– Kahlil Gibran

MARCH

2ND

March

If we could see the miracle
of a single flower clearly,
our whole life would change.

– Attributed to Buddha

3RD

March

The garden of the world has no limits,
except in your mind.

– Jalal al-Din Rumi

4TH

March

Study how water flows in a valley stream, smoothly and freely between the rocks. Also learn from holy books and wise people. Everything – even mountains, rivers, plants and trees – should be your teacher.

– Morihei Ueshiba

5TH

March

The little streams are noisy, but silent flow the great rivers.

– Buddha

6TH

March

When you inhale, you are taking
the strength from God.
When you exhale, it represents the service
you are giving to the world.

– B. K. S. Iyengar

7TH

March

Life is a series of natural
and spontaneous changes. Don't resist
them; that only creates sorrow.

– Lao Tzu

8TH

March

Every morning we are born again.
What we do today is
what matters most.

– *Buddha*

9TH

March

Let go of your mind
and then be mindful.
Close your ears and listen!

– *Jalal al-Din Rumi*

10TH

March

Men argue, nature acts.

– Voltaire

11TH

March

Let things flow naturally forward
in whatever way they like.

– *Lao Tzu*

12TH

March

In nature there are neither rewards
nor punishments – there are consequences.

– Robert Green Ingersoll

13TH

March

What a mistake has been to move
away from nature! In its variety, beauty,
cruelty, in its infinite and incomparable
greatness it holds the true meaning of life.

– Tiziano Terzani

14TH

March

Serenity of thought, gentleness,
silence, self-control, and purity
of purpose – all these are declared
as austerity of the mind.

– Bhagavad Gita

15TH

March

Before you speak, ask yourself:
is it kind, is it necessary, is it true,
does it improve the silence?

– Sathya Sai Baba

16TH

March

We read the world wrong and say that it deceives us.

– Rabindranath Tagore

17TH

March

If you walk, just walk. If you sit, just sit;
but whatever you do, don't wobble.

– Zen proverb

18TH

March

Only those who dare may fly.

– Luis Sepúlveda

19TH

March

You believe that everything is over,
but then there is always a robin
who starts singing.

– Paul Claudel

20TH

March

One must ask children and birds
how cherries and strawberries taste.

– Johann Wolfgang Goethe

21ST

March

It is spring again. The earth is like
a child that knows poems by heart.

– Rainer Maria Rilke

22ND

March

Like dawn my soul rises within me,
naked and unencumbered.

– Kahlil Gibran

23RD

March

You cannot cross the sea merely by standing
and staring at the water.

– Rabindranath Tagore

24TH

March

Man cannot discover new oceans unless
he has the courage to lose sight of the shore.

– André Gide

25TH

March

In the blossoming of a single flower,
the whole of the world is blooming.

– Zenrin-kushū

26TH

March

It is not easy to walk alone
in the country without musing
upon something.

– Charles Dickens

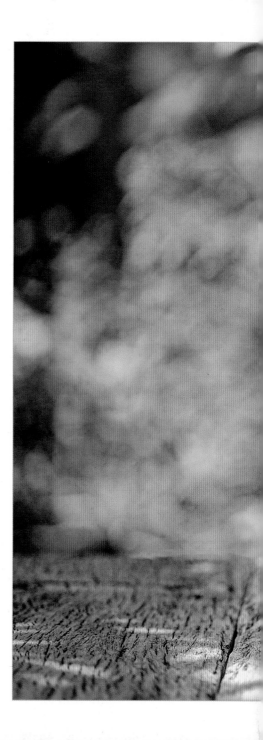

27TH

March

Joy can still be found in eating sparingly,
drinking plain water and using
the upper arm for a pillow.

– Confucius

28TH

March

Choose to be optimistic,
it feels better.

– Tenzin Gyatso, 14th Dalai Lama

29TH

March

The humblest tasks get beautified
if loving hands do them.

– Louisa May Alcott

30TH
March

If you possess happiness, you possess
everything; to be happy is to be
in tune with God.

– Paramahansa Yogananda

31ST
March

I have found that if you love life,
life will love you back.

– Arthur Rubinstein

1ST

April

Whoever stills sustained thoughts – as rain would, a cloud of dust –
through an awareness with thinking stilled, attains right here
the state of peace.

– Itivuttaka

APRIL

2ND

April

The ground you can change. Rip out the grass, level the hills,
pour a city over it. But rip out the wind?

– Richard Bach

3RD

April

Whoever tries to own a flower, will see its beauty withering.
But whoever just looks at a flower in a field, will remain with it forever.

– Paulo Coelho

4TH

April

In nature everything speaks, despite its apparent silence.

– Hazrat Inayat Khan

5TH

April

The flower hides in the grass, but the wind will carry its fragrance.

– Rabindranath Tagore

6TH

April

When you like a flower,
you just pluck it. But when you love
a flower, you water it daily.

– Attributed to Buddha

7TH

April

Children, old people, vagabonds laugh
easily and heartily: they have nothing
to lose and hope for little.

– Matthieu Ricard

8TH

April

For every cloud engenders not a storm.

– William Shakespeare

9TH

April

Patience is the key to heaven.

– Turkish proverb

10TH

April

I buy rice to live and I buy flowers
to have something to live for.

– Confucius

11TH

April

Why let go of yesterday?
Because yesterday has already
let go of you.

– Steve Maraboli

12TH

April

Mindfulness is present-moment awareness.
It takes place in the here and now.
It is the observance of what is happening
right now, in the present.

– Henepola Gunaratana

13TH

April

The sea has no country, either, and belongs to whoever will pause
to listen to it, here or there, wherever the sun dies or is born.

— Giovanni Verga

14TH

April

We may have all come on different ships,
but we're in the same boat now.

– Martin Luther King Jr.

15TH
April

Every flower is a soul blossoming
in nature.

– *Gérard de Nerval*

16TH
April

Look at the flowers – for no reason.
It is simply unbelievable
how happy flowers are.

– *Osho*

17TH

April

Green calm below, blue quietness above.

– John Greenleaf Whittier

18TH

April

You don't have to see the whole staircase,
just take the first step.

– Martin Luther King Jr.

19TH

April

Where there is quiet and meditation there is neither solicitude nor dissipation.

– Francis of Assisi

20TH

April

When you don't flow freely with life in the present moment, it usually means that you're holding on to a past moment.

– Louise Hay

21ˢᵀ

April

Fearlessness presupposes calmness
and peace of mind.

– Mahatma Gandhi

22ᴺᴰ

April

Never say there is nothing beautiful
in the world anymore. There is always
something to make you wonder
in the shape of a tree,
the trembling of a leaf.

– Albert Schweitzer

23RD

April

It is by harmonizing differences
that the world works, reproduces itself,
maintains its tension, lives.

– *Tiziano Terzani*

24TH

April

When I planted my pain in the field
of patience it bore fruit of happiness.

– *Kahlil Gibran*

25TH

April

To be beautiful means to be yourself.
You don't need to be accepted
by others. You need to accept yourself.

– *Thích Nhất Hạnh*

26TH

April

Love the animals, love the plants,
love everything. If you love everything,
you will perceive the divine mystery
in things.

– *Fyodor Dostoyevsky*

27TH

April

The flowers of spring are the dreams
of winter told, in the morning,
at the table of angels.

– Kahlil Gibran

28TH

April

Get moments of inner calm
and in these moments learn
to distinguish the essential
from the non-essential.

– Rudolf Steiner

29TH

April

Learn to be calm
and you will always be happy.

– *Paramahansa Yogananda*

30TH

April

Love is harmony. And happiness,
harmony, and well-being only blossom
from love. Learn to love.

– *Osho*

1ST

May

The fragrance of a flower spreads only in the direction of wind,
but a goodness of a person spreads in all directions.

– Chanakya

2ND

May

Beautify your inner world
with love light and compassion.

– Amit Ray

3RD

May

Movement overcomes cold;
stillness overcomes heat. Stillness
and tranquility set things in order
in the universe.

– Lao Tzu

4TH

May

Sunset is so marvelous that even the sun itself watches it
every day in the reflections of the infinite oceans!

– *Mehmet Murat Ildan*

5ᵀᴴ

May

Every sunset brings the promise
of a new dawn.

– *Ralph Waldo Emerson*

6TH

May

I yearn for flowers that bend with the wind and rain.

– *Zisi*

7TH

May

All things by immortal power, near or far, hiddenly, to each other linked are,
That thou canst not stir a flower, without troubling of a star.

– Francis Thompson

8TH

May

Walk slow, don't rush.
That place you have to reach is yourself.

– José Ortega y Gasset

9TH

May

As you explore the outer world,
your insight becomes deeper,
your intelligence becomes sharper,
your awareness becomes keener.

– Osho

10TH

May

Look well into thyself; there is a source
of strength which will always spring up
if thou wilt always look.

– Marcus Aurelius

11TH

May

Treat every moment as your last.
It is not preparation for something else.

– Shunryū Suzuki

12TH

May

After every storm the Sun will smile;
for every problem there is a solution,
and the soul's indefeasible duty
is to be of good cheer.

– William Rounseville Alger

13TH

May

Compassion for others begins
with kindness to ourselves.

– Pema Chödrön

14TH

May

It is indeed a radical act of love
just to sit down and be quiet
for a time by yourself.

– Jon Kabat-Zinn

15TH
May

Nature always wears the colours
of the spirit.

– Ralph Waldo Emerson

16TH
May

Stop, once in a while, and let
the wonder of the world possess you.

– Tiziano Terzani

17TH

May

Look at the trees, look at the birds, look at the clouds,
look at the stars ... and if you have eyes,
you will be able to see that the whole existence is joyful.

– Osho

18TH

May

Life is nothing but the continuous
wonder of existing.

– Rabindranath Tagore

19TH

May

The kindly search for growth,
the gracious desire to exist
of the flowers, my near ecstasy
at existing among them.

– *Allen Ginsberg*

20TH

May

Our task must be to free ourselves
by widening our circle of compassion
to embrace all living creatures
and the whole of nature and its beauty.

– Albert Einstein

21ST

May

If you are patient in one moment
of anger, you will avoid one hundred
days of sorrow.

– Chinese proverb

22ND

May

God grows weary of great kingdoms,
but never of little flowers.

– Rabindranath Tagore

23RD

May

Stretching his hand up to reach the stars,
too often man forgets the flowers at his feet.

– Jeremy Bentham

24TH

May

Look at nature from this meadow,
look at it intensely, and listen.

– Tiziano Terzani

25TH

May

The hour that's past never can return.

– Ovid

26TH

May

Each situation, each moment, is of infinite worth;
for each represents a whole eternity.

– Johann Wolfgang Goethe

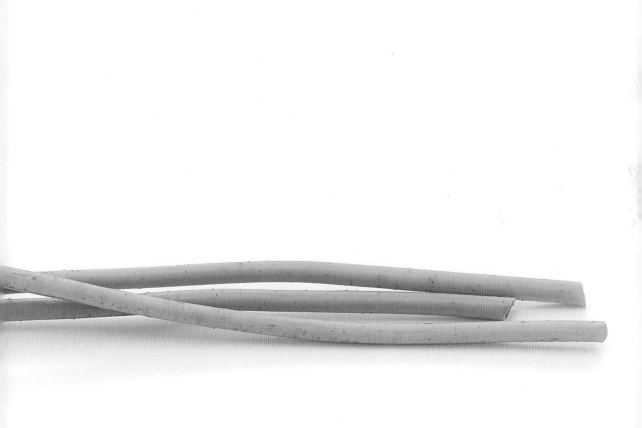

27TH

May

Until he extends the circle
of his compassion to all living things,
man will not himself find peace.

– Albert Schweitzer

28TH

May

How you treat yourself sets the standard
for how others will treat you.

– Steve Maraboli

29TH

May

To sit in the shade on a fine day
and look upon verdure is the most
perfect refreshment.

– Jane Austen

30TH

May

I don't try to help the lotus be a rose.
The world is rich because there is variety.

– Osho

31ST

May

May we exist like the lotus.
At ease in the muddy water.

– Zen prayer

1ST

June

Forget not that the earth delights to feel your bare feet
and the winds long to play with your hair.

– Kahlil Gibran

JUNE

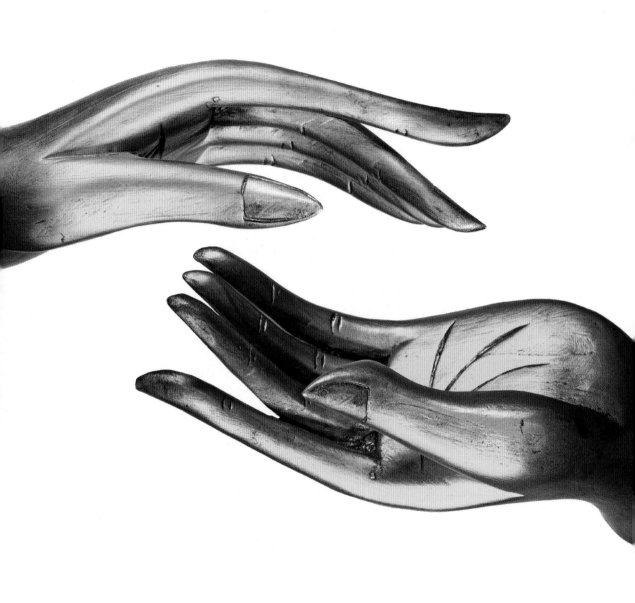

2ND

June

For it is in giving that we receive.

– Francis of Assisi

3RD

June

To walk safely through the maze
of human life, one needs the light
of wisdom and the guidance of virtue.

– Buddha

4TH

June

Calmness gives the devotee power to overcome all obstacles in life.

– Paramahansa Yogananda

5TH

June

There is no stone on your path on which you cannot step
to help your growth.

– Anonymous

6TH

June

If we are peaceful, if we are happy, we can smile and blossom
like a flower.

– Thích Nhất Hạnh

7TH

June

Green was the silence, wet was the light, the month of June
trembled like a butterfly.

– Pablo Neruda

8TH

June

Even the smallest feline is a masterpiece
of nature.

– Leonardo da Vinci

9TH

June

Each time I pass in front of a blossoming
almond tree I take my hat off.

– Ermanno Olmi

10TH

June

A single rose can be my garden ...
a single friend, my world.

– Leo Buscaglia

11TH

June

Stop and smell the roses.

– Proverb

12TH

June

Let the stillness direct
your words and actions.

– Eckhart Tolle

13TH

June

The simple things are also
the most extraordinary ones,
and only the wise can see them.

– Paulo Coelho

14TH

June

Start now, from where you stand.
Use what you have. Do the best you can.
What other philosophy of life
should you need?

– Zen proverb

15TH

June

Eternity. It is the sea mingled with the Sun.

– *Arthur Rimbaud*

16TH

June

The sea has this power: after a while,
it gives everything back, above all recollections.

– Carlos Ruiz Zafón

17TH

June

When someone knocks at your door,
never ask him, "Who are you?" Tell him: "Come and sit."

– Siberian proverb

18TH

June

Do little things now;
so shall big things come to thee
by and by asking to be done.

– Persian proverb

19TH

June

The flowering of meditation
is goodness, and the generosity
of the heart is the beginning
of meditation.

– Jiddu Krishnamurti

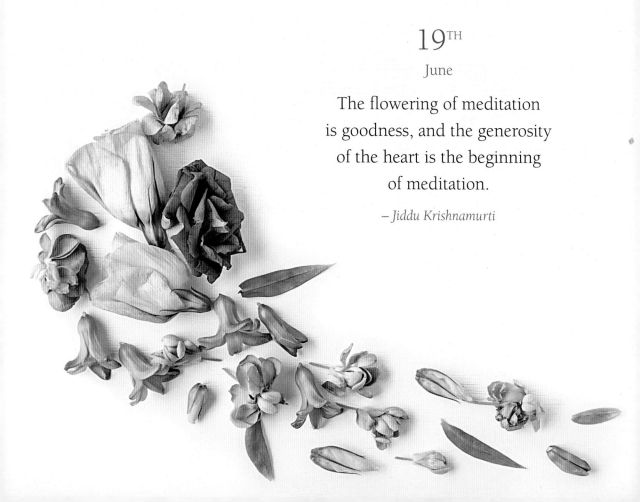

20TH

June

An orchid in a deep forest
sends out its fragrance even
if no one is around to appreciate it.

– Confucius

21ST

June

We shall never know all the good
that a simple smile can do.

– Mother Teresa

22ND

June

Let there be kindness in your face,
in your eyes, in your smile,
in the warmth of your greeting.

– Mother Teresa

23RD

June

There are always flowers
for those who want to see them.

– Henri Matisse

24TH

June

I live in a very small house,
but my windows look out
on a very large world.

– Confucius

25TH

June

Alone we can do so little;
together we can do so much.

– Helen Keller

26TH

June

Whenever you deeply accept
this moment as it is – no matter
what form it takes – you are still,
you are at peace.

– Eckhart Tolle

27TH

June

A superior man is calm
without being arrogant.

– *Confucius*

28TH

June

If you meet an enlightened man in the
street, do not greet him with words,
nor with silence.

– *Zen proverb*

29TH

June

When meditation is mastered,
the mind is unwavering like the flame
of a lamp in a windless place.

– *Bhagavadgītā*

30TH

June

Nirvana is not the blowing out
of the candle. It is the extinguishing
of the flame because day is come.

– *Rabindranath Tagore*

1ST

July

Remember to look up at the stars and not down at your feet ...
However difficult life may seem, there is always something
you can do and succeed at.

– Stephen Hawking

JULY

2ND

July

In the heart purified by friendship,
one beholds an open door of unity.

– Paramahansa Yogananda

3RD

July

Wishing to be friends is quick work,
but friendship is a slow ripening fruit.

– Aristotle

4TH

July

Just one ray of sunshine is enough
to dispel millions of shadows.

– Francis of Assisi

5TH

July

Bloom where you have been sown.

– Japanese proverb

6TH

July

Keep your face to the Sun
and you will never see the shadows.

– Helen Keller

7TH

July

I experience ecstasies, enjoyments inexpressible; it is then, that rushing
as it were into the great system of beings, I assimilate with universal Nature.

– Jean-Jacques Rousseau

8TH

July

The most powerful art in life
is to transform pain into a healing
talisman. A butterfly is reborn,
blossomed into a colorful party.

– Frida Kahlo

9TH

July

Ordinary people merely think
how they shall "spend" their time;
a man of talent tries to "use" it.

– Arthur Schopenhauer

10TH

July

A better planet is a dream
that begins to come true when
each of us decides to improve himself.

– Mahatma Gandhi

11TH

July

Patience is waiting. Don't wait passively.
This is laziness. But keep going
when the path is difficult and slow.

– Leo Tolstoy

12TH

July

There is no greatness where simplicity,
goodness, and truth are absent.

– Leo Tolstoy

13TH

July

Mindfulness of mind suggests a sense
of presence and a sense of accuracy
in terms of being there.

– Chögyam Trungpa

14TH

July

You are what existence wants you to be.
Just relax.

– Osho

15TH

July

Start the day with love, spend the day
with love, fill the day with love
and end the day with love.

– Sathya Sai Baba

16TH

July

Every child is an artist. The problem is
how to remain an artist once he grows up.

– Pablo Picasso

17TH

July

Each day is a little life.

– Arthur Schopenhauer

18TH

July

Mindfulness is living the present
time in full. It is the awareness
of what is happening right now,
without conceptualizing it.

– *Henepola Gunaratana*

19TH

July

Memories and thoughts age,
just as people do. But certain
thoughts can never age, and certain
memories can never fade.

– *Haruki Murakami*

20TH

July

There is in the day a serene hour
that can be defined as the absence of noise,
the serene hour of twilight.

– Victor Hugo

21ST

July

Far away there in the sunshine
are my highest aspirations.

– Louisa May Alcott

22ND

July

Live in the sunshine, swim the sea,
drink the wild air's salubrity.

– *Ralph Waldo Emerson*

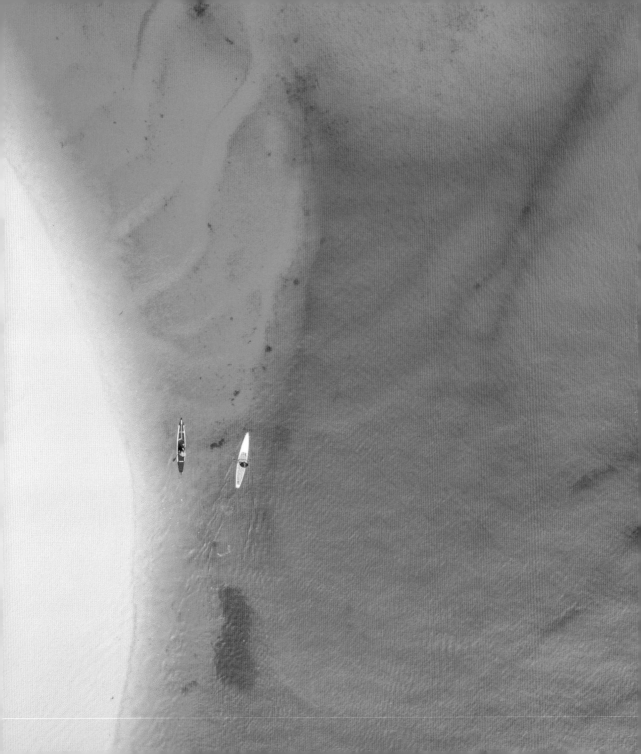

23RD

July

Raise your words, not your voice.
It is the rain that grows flowers,
not the thunder.

– Jalal al-Din Rumi

24TH

July

We forget that the water cycle
and the life cycle are one.

– Jacques-Yves Cousteau

25TH

July

Storms make the flowers fresh again.

– Charles Baudelaire

26TH

July

To enjoy the rainbow,
first enjoy the rain.

– Paulo Coelho

27TH

July

Storms don't come to teach us painful lessons, rather they were meant to wash us clean.

– Shannon L. Alder

28TH

July

The more violent the storm, the quicker it passes.

– Paulo Coelho

29TH

July

Nature is great in her great things, but even greater in her small ones.

– Attributed to Pliny the Elder

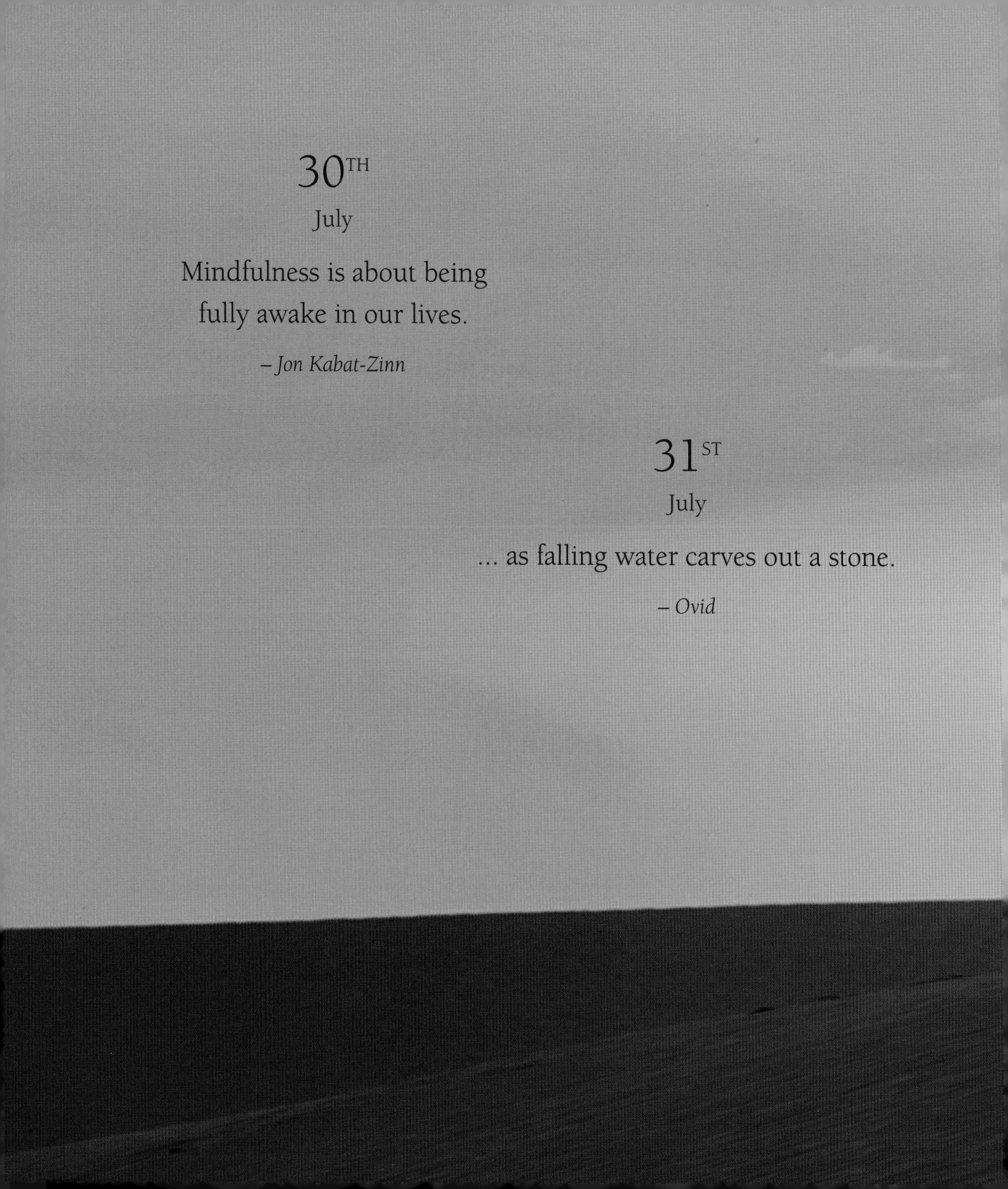

30TH

July

Mindfulness is about being
fully awake in our lives.

– Jon Kabat-Zinn

31ST

July

... as falling water carves out a stone.

– Ovid

1ST

August

If you wish to know the divine, feel the wind on your face
and the warm sun on your hand.

– Eido Tai Shimano

AUGUST

2ND

August

Every wall is a gate.

– *Ralph Waldo Emerson*

3RD

August

The way out is through the door.
Why is it that no one will use
this method?

– *Confucius*

4ᵀᴴ

August

Two voices are there; one is of the sea,
One of the mountains:
each a mighty Voice.

– *William Wordsworth*

5ᵀᴴ

August

For the breath of life is in the sunlight
and the hand of life is in the wind.

– *Kahlil Gibran*

6TH

August

It is like taking the Sun out of the world,
to bereave human life of friendship.

– Marcus Tullius Cicero

7TH

August

Let's learn to tolerate
and appreciate differences.

– Margherita Hack

8TH

August

The wild nature contains answers
to questions that man hasn't learned
to ask.

– Nancy Newhall

9TH

August

All the variety, all the charm,
all the beauty of life is made up of light
and shadow.

– Leo Tolstoy

10TH

August

The Sun shines for everybody.

– Latin proverb

11TH
August

Don't sit and wait. Get out there, feel life.
Touch the sun, and immerse in the sea.

– Jalal al-Din Rumi

12TH
August

Be like the cliff against which the waves
continually break; but it stands firm
and tames the fury of the water around it.

– Marcus Aurelius

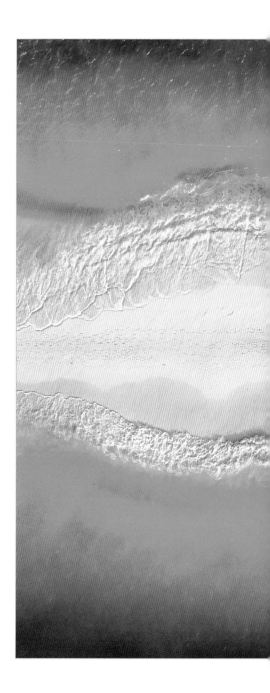

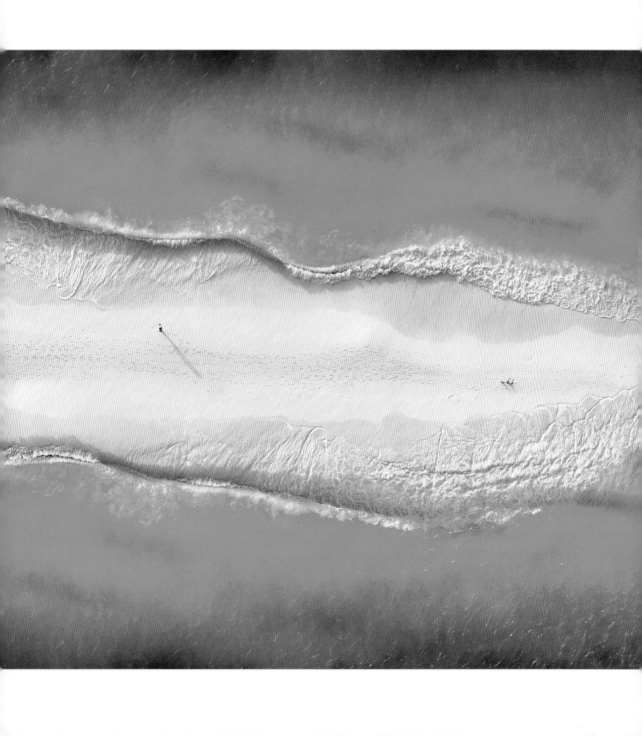

13TH

August

Choose only one Master – Nature.

– Rembrandt Harmenszoon van Rijn

14TH

August

I paint flowers so they will not die.

– Frida Kahlo

15TH

August

The sea reminds us that we are part
of a far greater design.

– *Anonymous*

16TH

August

Be an opener of doors
for such as come after thee.

– *Ralph Waldo Emerson*

17TH
August

And into the forest I go to lose my mind
and find my soul.

– John Muir

18TH
August

The farther I set my foot into this forest,
The more I feel in me calm and joy.

– Vittorio Alfieri

19TH

August

You are only afraid if you are not
in harmony with yourself.

– Hermann Hesse

20TH

August

You don't get rid of something
by avoiding it, but only by going
through it.

– Cesare Pavese

21ST
August

Water is the force that energizes you,
you will find yourself in water
and it will renew you.

– Eugenio Montale

22ND
August

So my mind sinks in this immensity:
and foundering is sweet in such a sea.

– Giacomo Leopardi

23RD

August

Colours are the smiles of nature.

– Leigh Hunt

24TH

August

Take rest; a field that has rested gives a plentiful crop.

– Ovid

25TH
August

Is it worth it for a child to learn
while crying when they could learn
while laughing?

– Gianni Rodari

26TH
August

Everything must come from the heart,
like a sudden gust of wind.

– Romano Battaglia

27TH
August

A Warrior of Light values a child's eyes
because they are able to look
at the world without bitterness.

– Paulo Coelho

28TH

August

Remember that sometimes not getting
what you want is a wonderful stroke
of luck.

– Tenzin Gyatso, the 14th Dalai Lama

29TH

August

We must envy no one; for the good
do not deserve envy and as for the
bad, the more they prosper, the more
they ruin themselves.

– *Epicurus*

30TH
August

Give every day the chance to become
the most beautiful day of your life.

— *Mark Twain*

31ST
August

There is one spectacle grander
than the sea, that is the sky;
there is one spectacle grander than the sky,
that is the interior of the soul.

— *Victor Hugo*

1ST

September

When I would recreate myself, I seek the darkest wood,
the thickest and most impenetrable and to the citizen, most dismal,
swamp. I enter a swamp as a sacred place, a sanctum sanctorum ...
this vast, savage, howling Mother of ours, Nature.

– Henry David Thoreau

SEPTEMBER

2ND

September

The mist that drifts away at dawn,
leaving but dew in the fields,
shall rise and gather into a cloud
and then fall down in rain.
And not unlike the mist have I been.

– Kahlil Gibran

3RD

September

Help your brother's boat across,
and your own will reach the shore.

– Hindu proverb

4ᵀᴴ

September

If the doors of perception were cleansed, everything
would appear to man as it is, infinite.

– William Blake

5ᵀᴴ

September

Let's try to live in peace, whatever our origin, belief,
color of skin, language and traditions might be.

– Margherita Hack

6TH

September

This happiness is to be with Nature,
to see, to hear, and to talk with her.

– *Leo Tolstoy*

7TH

September

Make like a tree. Change your opinions,
but keep to your principles; change
your leaves, but keep intact your roots.

– *Victor Hugo*

8TH

September

It only takes a reminder to breathe, a moment to be still, and just like that, something in me settles, softens, makes space for imperfection.

– *Danna Faulds*

9TH
September

There is nothing to fear in life,
but only something to understand.

– Margherita Hack

10TH
September

You must find the place inside yourself
where nothing is impossible.

– Deepak Chopra

11TH

September

Am I then really all that which other
men tell of? Or am I only
what I myself know of myself?

– Dietrich Bonhoeffer

12TH

September

The greatest happiness?
Being useful to others.

– Mother Teresa

13TH

September

In life, growing up means
growing deep within yourself –
that is where your roots are.

– *Osho*

14TH

September

Life is a great big canvas;
throw all the paint you can at it.

– *Danny Kaye*

15TH
September

Now I see the secret of the making
of the best persons.
It is to grow in the open air and to eat
and sleep with the earth.

– Walt Whitman

16TH
September

Compassion for animals is intimately
associated with goodness of character.

– Arthur Schopenhauer

17TH

September

We all have a common origin
in the evolution of the Universe
and the stars, so we can say to be
brothers and sisters.

– Margherita Hack

18TH

September

The butterfly counts not
months but moments,
and has time enough.

– Rabindranath Tagore

19TH
September

I am not afraid of storms, for I am
learning how to sail my ship.

– Louisa May Alcott

20TH
September

The more drops of clean water
there are, the more the beauty
of the world will shine.

– Mother Teresa

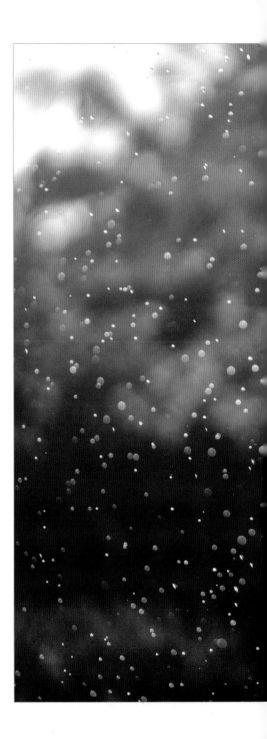

21ST

September

The secret of health for both mind
and body is not to mourn for the past,
nor to worry about the future,
but to live the present wisely and earnestly.

– Buddha

22ND

September

Believe there are no limits but the sky.

– Miguel de Cervantes

23RD

September

The real voyage of discovery consists not in seeking
new landscapes, but in having new eyes.

– Marcel Proust

24TH

September

I still see horizons where you draw borders.

– Frida Kahlo

25TH

September

Our every breath, every step we take,
can be full of peace, joy and serenity.

– *Thích Nhất Hạnh*

26TH

September

Each of us must learn to work not just
for his or her own self, family or nation,
but for the benefit of all mankind.

– Tenzin Gyatso, the 14th Dalai Lama

27TH

September

Difficulties break some men
but make others.

– Nelson Mandela

28TH

September

Make your heart like a lake,
with calm, still surface and great
depths of kindness.

– Lao Tzu

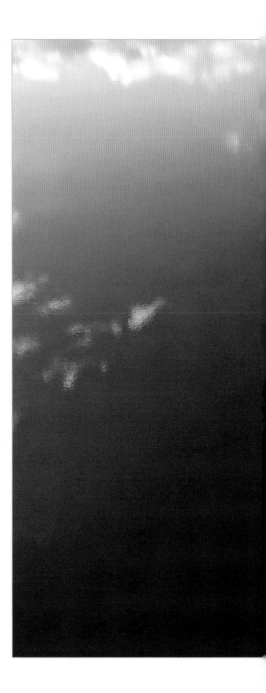

29TH

September

Appreciate life. It is from the silent
acceptance of it that energy comes.

– Deepak Chopra

30TH

September

Friendship and love are not asked
for like water, but are offered like tea.

– Zen proverb

1ST

October

There is a hidden message in every waterfall.
It says if you are flexible, falling will not hurt you.

– Mehmet Murat Ildan

OCTOBER

2ND

October

Forgive others not because they deserve
forgiveness, but because you deserve peace.

– Buddha

3RD

October

Aim for the Moon. If you miss,
you may hit a star.

– W. Clement Stone

4TH

October

Don't try to shine like jade,
but be as simple as stone.

– Lao Tzu

5TH

October

Our lack of confidence is not the result
of difficulty. The difficulty comes
from our lack of confidence.

– Lucius Annaeus Seneca

6TH

October

I close my eyes, think positive thoughts,
and breathe goodness in and out.

– Louise Hay

7TH

October

Great things are done when men
and mountains meet.

– William Blake

8TH

October

Water is the softest thing, yet it can penetrate
mountains and earth. This shows clearly the principle
of softness overcoming hardness.

– Lao Tzu

9TH

October

Our life, exempt from public haunt,
finds tongues in trees, books in the running brooks,
sermons in stones, and good in everything.

– William Shakespeare

10TH

October

One blissful moment whilst we live
weighs more than ages of renown.

– Voltaire

11TH

October

Thus ought recreation sometimes
to be given to the mind, that it may
return to you better fitted for thought.

– Phaedrus

12TH

October

Dogs are our link to paradise.
They don't know evil or jealousy
or discontent.

– Milan Kundera

13TH

October

Disciplined and calm, to await the
appearance of disorder and hubbub:
this is the art of retaining self-possession.

– *Sun Tzu*

14TH

October

Beautiful as a dandelion-blossom
golden in the green grass,
this life can be.

– Edna St. Vincent Millay

15TH

October

From the tree of silence hangs its fruit,
peace.

– Arthur Schopenhauer

16TH

October

Be like a tree. The tree gives shade
even to him who cuts off its boughs.

– Sri Chaitanya

17TH

October

It is more difficult to understand the works of nature
than those of a poet.

– Leonardo da Vinci

18TH

October

Fix your course on a star
and you'll navigate any storm.

– *Leonardo da Vinci*

19TH

October

Wake up! Be careful,
do not waste your life.

– Eihei Dōgen

20TH

October

Feelings come and go
like clouds in a windy sky.
Conscious breathing is my anchor.

– Thích Nhất Hạnh

21ST

October

There can be no very black melancholy
to him who lives in the midst of Nature
and has his senses still.

– *Henry David Thoreau*

22ND

October

Nature is not a place to visit.
It is home.

– *Gary Snyder*

23RD
October

Man does not know more than other
animals; he knows less. They know
what they need to know. We do not.

– Fernando Pessoa

24TH
October

Disinterested love for all living creatures,
the most noble attribute of man.

– Charles Darwin

25TH
October

We do not see nature with our eyes,
but with our understandings
and our hearts.

– William Hazlitt

26TH

October

Nothing awakens a memory
like a smell.

– Victor Hugo

27TH

October

A bath refreshes the body,
tea refreshes the mind.

– Japanese proverb

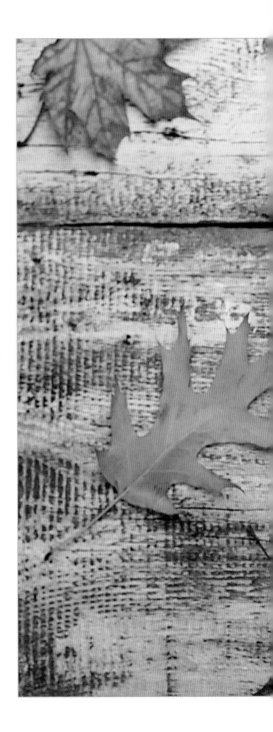

28TH

October

Happiness is love, nothing else.
Happy is who knows how to love.

– Hermann Hesse

29TH

October

Every child is in a way a genius;
and every genius is in a way a child.

– Arthur Schopenhauer

30TH
October

It's all vanity, it's all an illusion,
everything except that infinite sky.

– Leo Tolstoy

31ST
October

Always try to keep a patch of sky
above your life.

– Marcel Proust

1ST

November

The more one lives alone on the river or in the open country,
the clearer it becomes that nothing is more beautiful or great
than to perform the ordinary duties of one's daily life simply
and naturally. From the grasses in the field to the stars in the sky,
each one is doing just that; and there is such profound peace
and surpassing beauty in Nature because none of these tries forcibly
to transgress its limitations.

– Rabindranath Tagore

NOVEMBER

2ND

November

Time solves most things.
And what time can't solve,
you have to solve yourself.

– Haruki Murakami

3RD

November

Not thinking about anything is Zen.
Once you know this, walk,
sit or lie down, all you do is Zen.

– Bodhidharma

4TH

November

Be happy for this moment.
This moment is your life.

– Omar Khayyam

5TH

November

I let my whole being vibrate with light.

– Louise Hay

6TH

November

An early-morning walk is a blessing
for the whole day.

– Henry David Thoreau

7TH

November

What I see in Nature is a grand design that we can comprehend
only imperfectly, and that must fill a thinking person with a feeling of humility.

– Albert Einstein

8TH

November

Do not follow the ideas of others, but learn to listen
to the voice within yourself.

– *Eihei Dōgen*

9TH

November

The body is my temple,
asanas are my prayers.

– *B. K. S. Iyengar*

10TH

November

When there is effort,
there is no balance.

– *Osho*

11TH

November

We are friends. I want nothing from you.
And you want nothing from me.
We share life.

– Kahlil Gibran

12TH

November

Wherever you go, go with all your heart.

– Confucius

13TH

November

Health is the greatest possession. Contentment
is the greatest treasure. Confidence is the greatest friend.

– Lao Tzu

14TH

November

I decided to be happy. I heard it's good
for your health.

– Voltaire

15TH

November

A perfectly fulfilled man is one
who explores both the outer and the inner.

– *Osho*

16TH

November

Handle even a single leaf of a green
in such a way that it manifests the body
of the Buddha. This in turn allows
the Buddha to manifest
through the leaf.

– *Eihei Dōgen*

17TH

November

The best and most beautiful things
in the world cannot be seen or even
heard, but must be felt with the heart.

– *Helen Keller*

18TH

November

Happiness is not found at the top of the mountain, but in the way of climbing it.

– Confucius

19TH

November

The world is its own magic.

– Shunryū Suzuki

20TH
November

It's your road, and yours alone.
Others may walk it with you,
but no one can walk it for you.

– Zen proverb

21ST
November

The obstacle is the path.

– Zen proverb

22ND
November

We do not remember days,
we remember moments.

– Cesare Pavese

23RD

November

Wind and rivers bring a thousand
truths to mountains and trees.

– Beno Fignon

24TH

November

The clearest way into the Universe
is through a forest wilderness.

– John Muir

25TH

November

Every person takes the limits
of their own field of vision
for the limits of the world.

– Arthur Schopenhauer

26TH

November

Remember not the day that
has passed away from thee,
be not hard upon the morrow
that has not come,
think not about thine own
coming or departure,
drink wine now, and fling
not thy life to the winds.

– Omar Khayyam

27TH

November

A good traveler has no fixed plans
and is not intent upon arriving.

– Lao Tzu

28TH

November

If one has mind, nothing is ever lost,
regardless where one goes.

– Haruki Murakami

29TH

November

Bliss is balance.

– Osho

30TH

November

Friends are medicine for a wounded heart, and vitamins for a hopeful soul.

– Steve Maraboli

1ST

December

Wildness reminds us what it means to be human,
what we are connected to rather than what we are separate from.

– Terry Tempest Williams

DECEMBER

2ND

December

Wildness is the preservation
of the World.

– Henry David Thoreau

3RD

December

There is no snow as attractive
as the snow of the end of Shabbat.
What is that snow like?
Like the feathers of angels' wings.

– Shmuel Yosef Agnon

4TH

December

Relax. Concentrate. Dispel every other thought.
Let the world around you fade.

– *Italo Calvino*

5TH

December

It is only with the heart that one can see rightly;
what is essential is invisible to the eye.

– Antoine de Saint-Exupéry

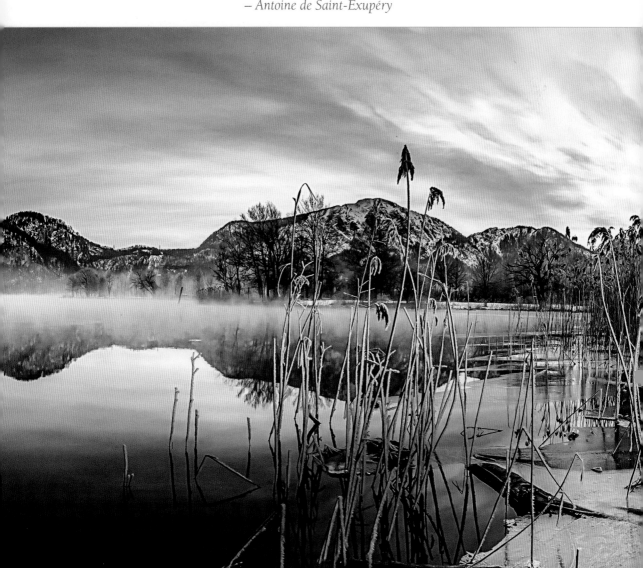

6TH

December

Some people talk to animals.
Not many listen though.
That's the problem.

– Alan Alexander Milne

7TH

December

Mindfulness isn't difficult, we just need
to remember to do it.

– Sharon Salzberg

8TH

December

When I was a child, I believed I had
a guardian angel beside me. Now I think
I have one within me.

– Erri De Luca

9TH

December

You are never too old to set another
goal or to dream a new dream.

— *Les Brown*

10TH

December

I live not in myself, but I become
portion of that around me: and to me
high mountains are a feeling.

— *Lord Byron*

11TH

December

When we realize the everlasting truth
of "everything changes" and find our composure
in it, we find ourselves in Nirvana.

– Shunryū Suzuki

12TH

December

For when a man has suffered much, and been buffeted
about in the world, he takes pleasure in recalling
the memory of sorrows that have long gone by.

– Homer

13TH

December

In every walk with Nature, one receives
far more than he seeks.

– John Muir

14TH

December

True friendship resists time,
distance, and silence.

– Isabel Allende

15TH

December

The mountains are mute teachers
and make silent disciples.

– Johann Wolfgang Goethe

16TH

December

Now I am drunk with universe.

– Giuseppe Ungaretti

17TH

December

Let us be grateful to people
who make us happy;
they are the charming gardeners
who make our souls blossom.

– *Marcel Proust*

18TH

December

No snowflake ever falls in the wrong place.

– Zen proverb

19TH

December

The river needs to take the risk of entering the ocean
because only then will fear disappear.

– Kahlil Gibran

20TH
December

The thought contains the possibility
of the state of affairs which it thinks.
What is thinkable is also possible.

– *Ludwig Wittgenstein*

21ST
December

The seasons are what a symphony
ought to be: four perfect movements
in harmony with each other.

– *Arthur Rubinstein*

22ND
December

A calf is still able to dream, this is the reason
why it sees a magic world,
one of which you lost sight.

– Sergio Bambarén

23RD

December

Love is every movement of our soul
where it feels itself and perceives
its own life.

– Hermann Hesse

24TH

December

Open your nostrils. Smell snow.
Let life happen.

– Sylvia Plath

25TH

December

Being like the flower; it is born, it opens and breathes peacefully,
sings under the sky, in the light, even if death still exists.

– Luis Cernuda

26TH

December

If we give each other a hand, miracles will happen,
and Christmas will last all year long.

– Gianni Rodari

27TH

December

To feel the presence of an angel is like feeling the wind all around you.
You cannot actually see the wind, but you feel it, and you know it is there.

– Bernard of Clairvaux

28TH

December

I believe that if one always looked
at the skies, one would end up
with wings.

– Gustave Flaubert

29TH

December

Life is a great adventure
toward the light.

– Paul Claudel

30TH

December

When we create peace, and harmony,
and balance in our minds,
we will find it in our lives.

– Louise Hay

31ST

December

Being born is not enough.
It is to be reborn that we are born.
Every day.

– Pablo Neruda

LIST OF CONTRIBUTORS

A

Abbey, Edward
(1927 - 1989)
American philosopher, writer,
and environmentalist.
(February 15th)

Agnon, Shmuel Yosef
(1888 - 1970)
Israeli writer and poet;
Nobel Prize in Literature in 1966.
(December 3rd)

Alcott, Louisa May
(1832 - 1888)
American writer.
(March 29th, July 21st, September 19th)

Alder, Shannon L.
(living)
American inspirational author.
(July 27th)

Alfieri, Vittorio
(1749 - 1803)
Italian poet and playwright.
(August 18th)

Alger, William Rounseville
(1822 - 1905)
American writer and poet.
(May 12th)

Allende, Isabel
(1942 - living)
Chilean-born American novelist.
(December 14th)

Anhava, Helena
(1925 - 2018)
Finnish author, poet, and translator.
(January 8th)

Anonymous
(June 5th, August 15th)

Aristotle
(384 BCE - 322 BCE)
Greek philosopher.
(January 19th, January 23rd,
February 3rd, July 3rd)

Austen, Jane
(1775 - 1817)
English novelist.
(May 29th)

B

Bach, Richard
(1936 - living)
American author and
aviator.
(April 2nd)

Bacon, Francis
(1561 - 1626)
English philosopher and statesman.
(January 5th)

Bambarén, Sergio
(1960 - living)
Peruvian-born Australian author.
(December 22nd)

Battaglia, Romano
(1933 - 2012)
Italian author and journalist.
(January 31st, February 9th, August 26th)

Baudelaire, Charles
(1821 - 1867)
French poet and literary critic.
(January 22nd, July 25th)

Beck, Charlotte Joko
(1917 - 2011)
American Zen teacher and author.
(January 7th)

Bentham, Jeremy
(1748 - 1832)
English philosopher.
(May 23rd)

Bernard of Clairvaux
(1090 - 1153)
French Christian monk
and theologian.
(January 3rd, December 27th)

Bhagavad Gita
Hindu holy scripture, dated to
the second half of the first
millennium BCE.
(March 14th, June 29th)

Blake, William
(1757 - 1827)
English poet, painter, and printmaker.
(September 4th, October 7th)

Bodhidharma
(c. 483 - 540)
Indian Buddhist monk, first patriarch
of Chinese Buddhism.
(November 3rd)

Bonhoeffer, Dietrich
(1906 - 1945)
German Lutheran pastor, theologian,
poet, and anti-Nazi dissident.
(September 11th)

Brown, Les
(1945 - living)
American author and motivational
speaker.
(December 9th)

Bryant, William Cullen
(1794 - 1878)
American poet and journalist.
(February 2nd)

Buddha
(566 BCE - 486 BCE)
Indian ascetic and spiritual teacher;
founder of Buddhism.
(January 14th, January 18th, January
26th, February 13th, March 2nd,
March 5th, March 8th, April 6th, June 3rd,
September 21st, October 2nd)

Buscaglia, Leo
(1924 - 1998)
American writer and teacher.
(June 10th)

Byron, Lord
(1788 - 1824)
English poet.
(December 10th)

C

Calvino, Italo
(1923 - 1985)
Italian writer and journalist.
(December 4th)

Camus, Albert
(1913 - 1960)
French author; Nobel Prize in
Literature in 1957.
(January 15th, February 26th)

Cernuda, Luis
(1902 - 1963)
Spanish poet.
(December 25th)

Cervantes, Miguel de
(1547 - 1616)
Spanish writer and poet.
(September 22nd)

(Sri) Chaitanya
(1486 - 1533)
Indian mystic.
(October 16th)

Chanakya
(371 BCE - 283 BCE)
Indian writer and poet.
(May 1st)

Chaplin, Charlie
(1889 - 1977)
English actor and director.
(February 7th)

Chinese proverb
(January 21st, May 21st)

Chödrön, Pema
(1936 - living)
American Buddhist nun and author.
(May 13th)

Chopin, Frédéric
(1810 - 1849)
Polish musician and composer.
(January 10th)

Chopra, Deepak
(1946 - living)
Indian physician and writer.
(September 10th, September 29th)

Cicero, Marcus Tullius
(106 BCE - 43 BCE)
Roman statesman and scholar.
(August 6th)

Claudel, Paul
(1868 - 1955)
French poet, playwright, and diplomat.
(March 19th, December 29th)

Coelho, Paulo
(1947 - living)
Brazilian writer and poet.
(January 25th, April 3rd, June 13th,
July 26th, July 28th, August 27th)

Confucius
(551 BCE - 479 BCE)
Chinese philosopher.
(January 12th, January 28th,
February 23rd, March 27th,
April 10th, June 20th, June 24th,
June 27th, August 3rd, November 12th,
November 18th)

Cousteau, Jacques-Yves
(1910 - 1997)
French naval officer, oceanographer,
and filmmaker.
(July 24th)

D

Darwin, Charles
(1809 - 1882)
English naturalist, geologist,
and biologist, best known for his
contributions to evolutionary biology.
(October 24th)

De Luca, Erri
(1950 - living)
Italian writer, poet, and journalist.
(January 17th, December 8th)

Dickens, Charles
(1812 - 1870)
English writer and social critic.
(March 26th)

Dōgen, Eihei
(1200 - 1253)
Japanese Buddhist monk, founder
of Zen Sōtō Buddhist school.
(January 24th, October 19th,
November 8th, November 16th)

Dostoyevsky, Fyodor
(1821 - 1881)
Russian writer.
(April 26th)

E
Einstein, Albert
(1879 - 1955)
German-born American and Swiss
theoretical physicist; Nobel Prize
in Physics in 1921.
(February 21st, February 22nd,
May 20th, November 7th)

Emerson, Ralph Waldo
(1803 - 1882)
American writer and philosopher.
(January 9th, May 5th, May 15th,
July 22nd, August 2nd, August 16th)

Epicurus
(341 BCE - 270 BCE)
Greek philosopher.
(February 25th, August 29th)

F
Faulds, Danna
(living)
American yoga teacher, poet,
and author.
(September 8th)

Fignon, Beno
(1946 - 2009)
Italian writer and musician.
(November 23rd)

Flaubert, Gustave
(1821 - 1880)
French writer.
(December 28th)

Francis of Assisi
(1181/1182 - 1226)
Italian Catholic friar, poet,
and mystic.
(April 19th, June 2nd, July 4th)

G
Galen
(c. 129 - 201)
Greek physician.
(February 12th)

Gandhi, Mahatma
(1869 - 1948)
Indian lawyer, statesman,
and philosopher.
(April 21st, July 10th)

Gibran, Kahlil
(1883 - 1931)
Lebanese writer and poet.
(February 4th, February 8th, March 1st,
March 22nd, April 24th, April 27th,
June 1st, August 5th, September 2nd,
November 11th, December 19th)

Gide, André
(1869 - 1951)
French writer; Nobel Prize in Literature
in 1947.
(March 24th)

Ginsberg, Allen
(1926 - 1997)
American writer and poet.
(May 19th)

Goethe, Johann Wolfgang
(1749 - 1832)
German writer and poet.
(February 5th, March 20th, May 26th,
December 15th)

Gunaratana, Henepola
(1927 - living)
Sri Lankan Theravada Buddhist monk
and author.
(April 12th, July 18th)

Gyatso, Tenzin
(1935 - living)
Tibetan Buddhist monk,
14th Dalai Lama.
(January 1st, January 30th,
February 24th, March 28th, August 28th,
September 26th)

H
Hack, Margherita
(1922 - 2013)
Italian astrophysicist, science
communicator, and activist.
(August 7th, September 5th,
September 9th, September 17th)

Hauge, Olav H.
(1908 - 1994)
Norwegian poet.
(January 2nd)

Hawking, Stephen
(1942 - 2018)
British theoretical physicist,
cosmologist, and mathematician.
(July 1st)

Hay, Louise
(1926 - 2017)
American writer.
(April 20th, October 6th,
November 5th, December 30th)

Hazlitt, William
(1778 - 1830)
English philosopher, literary critic,
and painter.
(October 25th)

Hesse, Hermann
(1877 - 1962)
German writer, poet, and
philosopher; Nobel Prize in
Literature in 1946.
(August 19th, October 28th,
December 23rd)

Hindu proverb
(September 3rd)

Hippocrates
(c. 460 BCE - 370 BCE)
Greek physician and geographer.
(February 11th)

Homer
(9th - 8th century BCE)
Greek poet.
(December 12th)

Hugo, Victor
(1802 - 1885)
French writer and poet.
(July 20th, August 31st, September 7th,
October 26th)

Hunt, Leigh
(1784 - 1859)
English writer and poet.
(August 23rd)

I
Ildan, Mehmet Murat
(1965 - living)
Turkish writer and playwright.
(May 4th, October 1st)

Inayat Khan, Hazrat
(1882 - 1927)
Indian mystic, musician, and writer.
(April 4th)

Ingersoll, Robert Green
(1833 - 1899)
American lawyer, writer, and orator.
(March 12th)

Itivuttaka
Buddhist scripture, part of the
Pali Canon of Theravada
Buddhism.
(April 1st)

**Iyengar, Bellur Krishnamachar
Sundararaja**
(1918 - 2014)
Indian mystic.
(March 6th, November 9th)

J
Japanese proverb
(July 5th, October 27th)

Jekyll, Gertrude
(1843 - 1932)
English writer and artist.
(February 27th)

Jesus of Nazareth
(c. 4 BCE - 30/33 CE)
Jewish religious leader, founder
of Christianity.
(February 16th)

K
Kabat-Zinn, Jon
(1944 - living)
American scholar, founder of the
Stress Reduction Clinic and the
Center for Mindfulness in Medicine,
Health Care and Society at the
University of Massachusetts Medical
School.
(May 14th, July 30th)

Kahlo, Frida
(1907 - 1954)
Mexican painter.
(July 8th, August 14th, September 24th)

Kaye, Danny
(1913 - 1987)
American actor, singer, comedian,
and ambassador-at-large of UNICEF.
(September 14th)

Keller, Helen
(1880 - 1968)
American writer and activist.
(June 25th, July 6th, November 17th)

Khayyam Omar
(1048 - 1131)
Persian astronomer, mathematician,
and poet.
(November 4th, November 26th)

King, Martin Luther, Jr.
(1929 - 1968)
American Baptist minister and civil
right activist.
(April 14th, April 18th)

Krishnamurti, Jiddu
(1895 - 1986)
Indian free thinker and author.
(June 19th)

Kundera, Milan
(1929 - living)
Czech-born French poet and
writer.
(October 12th)

L
Lao Tzu
(6th century BCE)
Chinese philosopher and
writer.
(March 7th, March 11th, May 3rd,
September 28th, October 4th,
October 8th, November 13th,
November 27th)

Latin proverb
(August 10th)

Steiner, Rudolf
(1861 - 1925)
Austrian social reformer and occultist.
(April 28th)

Stone, Clement W.
(1902 - 2002)
American businessman, philanthropist, and author.
(October 3rd)

Stout, Ruth
(1884 - 1980)
American horticulturist and author.
(January 11th)

Sun Tzu
(544 BCE - 496 BCE)
Chinese philosopher and strategist.
(October 13th)

Suzuki, Shunryū
(1904 - 1971)
Japanese Zen Sōtō Buddhist monk and author.
(May 11th, November 19th, December 11th)

T
Tagore, Rabindranath
(1861 - 1941)
Bengali poet, philosopher, playwright, and social reformer.
(March 16th, March 23rd, April 5th, May 18th, May 22nd, June 30th, September 18th, November 1st)

Terzani, Tiziano
(1938 - 2004)
Italian writer and journalist.
(February 19th, March 13th, April 23rd, May 16th, May 24th)

Thích Nhất Hạnh
(1926 - 2022)
Vietnamese Buddhist monk, peace activist, and author.
(February 20th, April 25th, June 6th, September 25th, October 20th)

Thomas à Kempis
(1380 - 1471)
German mystic and Christian monk.
(January 4th)

Thompson, Francis
(1859 - 1907)
English poet.
(May 7th)

Thoreau, Henry David
(1817 - 1862)
American philosopher, writer, and poet.
(January 27th, September 1st, October 21st, November 6th, December 2nd)

Tolle, Eckhart
(1948 - living)
German spiritual teacher and self-help author.
(June 12th, June 26th)

Tolstoy, Leo
(1828 - 1910)
Russian writer.
(July 11th, July 12th, August 9th, September 6th, October 30th)

Trungpa, Chögyam
(1939 - 1987)
Tibetan author, philosopher, and meditation master.
(July 13th)

Turkish proverb
(April 9th)

Twain, Mark
(1835 - 1910)
American writer and poet.
(August 30th)

U
Ueshiba Morihei
(1883 - 1969)
Japanese martial artist, founder of aikido.
(March 4th)

Ungaretti, Giuseppe
(1888 - 1970)
Italian poet.
(January 13th, February 10th, December 16th)

V
Van Dyke, Henry
(1852 - 1933)
American author, educator, and Presbyterian clergyman.
(January 6th, January 29th)

Verga, Giovanni
(1840 - 1922)
Italian writer.
(April 13th)

Voltaire
(1694 - 1778)
Nom de plume of François-Marie Arouet, French philosopher and writer.
(March 10th, October 10th, November 14th)

W
Walker, Alice
(1944 - living)
American writer, poet, and activist.
(January 16th)

Whitman, Walt
(1819 - 1892)
American poet and journalist.
(September 15th)

Whittier, John Greenleaf
(1807 - 1892)
American poet.
(April 17th)

Williams, Terry Tempest
(1955 - living)
American environmental activist and author.
(December 1st)

Wittgenstein, Ludwig
(1889 - 1951)
Austrian-born British philosopher.
(December 20th)

Wordsworth, William
(1770 - 1850)
English poet.
(August 4th)

Y
Yogananda, Paramahansa
(1893 - 1952)
Indian mystic and philosopher.
(March 30th, April 29th, June 4th, July 2nd)

Z
Zen prayer
(May 31st)

Zen proverb
(February 18th, March 17th, June 14th, June 28th, September 30th, November 20th, November 21st, December 18th)

Zenrin-kushū
Collection of writings used in the Rinzai school of Zen since the XV century CE.
(March 25th)

Zisi
(483 BCE - 402 BCE)
Chinese philosopher.
(May 6th)

PHOTO CREDITS

All images are from Shutterstock.com

Introduction
Manuela Perugini

Edited
GFB Edit, Sesto San Giovanni (MI)

Project Editor
Valeria Manferto De Fabianis

Graphic Designer
Paola Piacco

Editorial Coordination
Giorgio Ferrero

WS White Star Publishers® is a registered trademark property of White Star s.r.l.

© 2023 White Star s.r.l.
Piazzale Luigi Cadorna, 6
20123 Milan, Italy
www.whitestar.it

ISBN 978-88-544-1954-4
1 2 3 4 5 6   27 26 25 24 23

Printed in China